Table of Contents

FIGURE

Introduction

Hans Morgenthau, a founding father of the realist school of international politics, described foreign aid as "the continuation of diplomacy by other means."[1] In his political theory of foreign aid, Morgenthau argued that the United States has interests abroad that cannot be secured by military means or by traditional methods of diplomacy, and foreign aid is a means to support such interests.[2] As noted by Morgenthau, the aid giver can derive political loyalties from the recipient country when there is a positive relationship between the aid and its benefits with the political philosophy, system or objectives of the giver, i.e. foreign aid is ineffectual if the recipient believes "aid is good, but the politics of the giver is bad."[3] Morgenthau added that the political nature of foreign aid makes it more of an art than a science, requiring a mental predisposition toward the political sensitivity of the interrelationship among the facts, present and future, and ends and means. Morgenthau provided a realist perspective advocating that foreign aid should be considered another tool of national power to achieve strategic objectives.

In the era of the Global War on Terrorism, the United States used foreign aid to strengthen weak states in order to deny sanctuaries to terrorists, an important strategic objective.[4] With the end of the U.S. military mission in Iraq on December 15, 2011 and a proposed withdrawal of U.S. military forces from Afghanistan by 2014, the current policy debate is on preparing for a future in the midst of a large deficit in the U.S. budget. The competition for limited budgetary resources is fierce and the effectiveness of U.S. foreign aid at projecting U.S. influence is hotly debated within the government and the American public.

Carol Lancaster, Dean of the School of Foreign Service at Georgetown University, described the perspective of the other schools of international relations theories on foreign aid in in *Foreign Aid: Diplomacy, Development, Domestic Politics*.[5] Lancaster suggested that liberal internationalists would consider foreign aid to be an instrument of states to cooperate on problems of interdependence and globalization. Further, Lancaster asserted that constructivists might view foreign aid as the evolution in relations between states in which rich countries

---

[1] Hans Morgenthau, "Introductions," *The New Statecraft* by George Liska (Chicago; Univeristy of Chicago Press, 1960), iv.

[2] Hans Morgenthau, "A Political Theory of Foreign Aid," *The American Political Science Review* 56, no. 2 (June 1962), 301-309.

[3] Ibid.

[4] Carol Lancaster and Ann Van Dusen, *Organizing U.S. Foreign Aid: Confronting the Challenges of the 21st Century* (Washington, DC: Brookings Institution Press, 2005), 10.

[5] Carol Lancaster, *Foreign Aid: Diplomacy, Development, Domestic Politics* (Chicago, IL: University of Chicago Press, 2006), 3-4.

should provide assistance to improve the quality of life in poor countries. As an example of this perspective, Lancaster cited David Lumsdaine, political science professor at Gordon College, who argued that economic foreign aid cannot be explained on the basis of the political and economic interests of the donor states and that humanitarian concerns were at the foundation of support for foreign economic aid.[6]

The current U.S. policy on diplomacy and development could be interpreted as a combination of all three schools of international relations theories as described by Lancaster. The Executive Summary accompanying the fiscal year 2013 budget request from the Department of State stated that

> our investment in diplomacy and development supports efforts to secure American interests, strengthen our friends and allies, forge new partnerships and promote our values in every region of the globe.[7]

This statement combines the ideals of constructivism, where American values are promoted globally, with the motivation for strategic advantage by securing American interests espoused by realism and fostering partnerships and interdependence advocated by international liberalism. Elevating development as an instrument of national power was an initiative described in the September 2010 Presidential Policy Directive on U.S. Global Development, which called for a complementary and comprehensive approach to national security using development, diplomacy, and defense.[8] The identification of development as a tool of national power is similar to Morgenthau's concept of foreign aid.

The U.S. foreign aid program has its roots in the Marshall Plan, developed to counter communism in Europe and restore critical trade relationships vital to American manufacturing following World War II.[9] Constructivism, liberal internationalism, and realism were also apparent in the Marshall Plan, which addressed the devastation throughout Europe caused by the war; protection of American interests in the continent by countering communism; and strengthening and building relationships with allies. During the Cold War, the competition for influence in Asia, Middle East, Latin America, and Africa in the 1950s and 1960s ushered in the

---

[6] Ibid.

[7] U.S. Department of State, "FY 2013 Executive Budget Summary - Function 150 and Other International Programs, February 13, 2012," http://www.state.gov/s/d/rm/rls/ebs/2013/index.htm (accessed October 11, 2012).

[8] Office of the U.S. President, "Fact Sheet: U.S. Global Development Policy, September 22, 2010," http://www.whitehouse.gov/the-press-office/2010/09/22/fact-sheet-us-global-development-policy (accessed September 5, 2012).

[9] Lael Brainard, Security by Other Means: Foreign Assistance, Global Poverty, and American Leadership (Washington, DC: Brookings Institution Press, 2006), 2.

use of U.S. aid to alleviate suffering in developing countries, thereby preventing a communist foothold in these regions.[10] For example, during the Vietnam War, a war waged to counter communism in Indochina, White House Deputy Special Assistance for National Security Affairs Walt W. Rostow advised President John F. Kennedy and the U.S. military to combine development and reform with military action as part of the pacification program in South Vietnam.[11] Senior U.S. policy-makers during the Vietnam War considered development as an instrument of national power along with military action in strengthening the South Vietnamese government as well as a means to counter communism.

U.S. foreign aid later focused on building international institutions and promoting democracy. The U.S. Agency for International Development (USAID) was created in 1961 and the United States contributed significant funds to the World Bank and other multilateral aid agencies during the 1970s, strengthening international aid organizations.[12] After the Cold War, promoting democracy in the former Soviet Union became prominent. In March 1993, Senator Patrick Leahy called for a "major shift in funding priorities toward a bold new aid program to help Russia make the transition to democracy."[13]

Anecdotal evidence from previous studies suggests that foreign aid had mixed impact on the position of recipient countries toward U.S. political objectives. In a study on the United Nations voting outcomes on issues of importance to the United States, results showed that foreign aid programs were successfully used as a reward to induce favorable votes from United Nations members.[14] During the Cold War, the United States provided foreign aid and sponsored development programs in Nepal, which allowed U.S. officials to gain insights into the regional dynamics with Communist China.[15] However, the aid provided to Nepal did not measurably contain Communism or promote democracy because of the entrenched Communist loyalists in the Nepalese education community and the necessity of maintaining good relations with its monarchy. In addition, the distribution of aid coincided with U.S. political goals. During the

---

[10] Lancaster and Dusen, 10.

[11] Graham A. Cosmas, *MACV: The Joint Command in the Years of Escalation, 1962-1967, United States Army in Vietnam* (Washington, DC: United States Army Center of Military History, 2006), 17.

[12] Lancaster and Van Dusen, 10.

[13] U.S. Congress. *Congressional Record*. 103rd Congress, 1st Session, March 19, 1993. Vol. 139, No. 35: S3240-S3242. http://thomas.loc.gov/cgi-bin/query/D?r103:368:./temp/~r103Ydml6Z:: (accessed October 11, 2012).

[14] T. Y. Wang, "U.S. Foreign Aid and UN Voting: An Analysis of Important Issues," *International Studies Quarterly* 43, no. 1 (March 1999), 199-210.

[15] Narayan Khadka, "U.S. Aid to Nepal in the Cold War Period: Lessons for the Future," *Pacific Affairs* 73, no. 1 (Spring 2000), 77-95.

1980s, the United States allocated military aid primarily to countries that shared a border with a communist country or were in Central America, areas which were national security interest to the United States at the time.[16] During his administration, U.S. President Jimmy Carter exerted significant amount of attention and effort on securing a Middle East peace agreement, primarily through engagement with Israel and Egypt.[17] President Carter secured more agreements with Middle Eastern countries than any other U.S. administration since Carter's time, with Egypt and Israel receiving the majority of USAID projects. In addition, during the Cold War, foreign democratic governments were more likely to receive U.S. aid but the amount decreased after the Cold War.[18] Post-Cold War, security was an important factor in determining the recipient of U.S. aid.[19]

This research builds on these previous studies by examining the use of foreign aid as a U.S. foreign policy tool in Egypt and Israel through select historical examples from the 1950s and 1960s. The United States considers the Middle East stability to be a top national security priority, despite an elusive peace for the region. The United States maintains an "unshakable commitment" to Israel's security.[20] The United States considers Egypt to be an influential Arab voice in the region, especially in light of the Arab Spring Revolution.[21] In addition, Israel and Egypt play important roles in, and have influence on the Middle East peace process. The large amount of aid given to Israel and Egypt reflects the importance of the relationship with both countries to the United States. However, aid is not enough to guarantee a Middle East peace agreement, which remains as intangible as the day Israel declared its independence on May 14, 1948.

This research focused on the 1950s to 1960s period for Israel and Egypt because both countries were trying to establish their respective identities and regional roles at this time, with the United States and Soviet Union competing for influence in the area as well. U.S. foreign

---

[16] Steven C. Poe and James Meernik, "US Military Aid in the 1980s: A Global Analysis," *Journal of Peace Research* 32, no. 4 (November 1995), 399-411.

[17] Kiki Caruson and Victoria A. Farrar-Myers, "Promoting the President's Foreign Policy Agenda: Presidential Use of Executive Agreements as Policy Vehicles," *Political Research Quarterly* 60, no. 4 (December 2007), 631-644.

[18] James Meernik, Eric L. Krueger, Steven C. Poe, "Testing Models of U.S. Foreign Policy: Foreign Aid during and after the Cold War," *The Journal of Politics* 60, no. 1 (February 1998), 63-85.

[19] Brian Lai, "Examining the Goals of US Foreign Assistance in the Post-Cold War Period, 1991-96," *Journal of Peace Research* 40, no. 1 (January 2003), 103-128.

[20] Barack Obama, *National Security Strategy*, Washington, DC: The White House, 2010.

[21] U.S. Department of State, "Fact Sheet: U.S.-Relations with Egypt, August 22, 2012," http://www.state.gov/r/pa/ei/bgn/5309.htm (accessed September 6, 2012).

policy actions during this time period were important in establishing the foundation of the relationships between these two countries with the United States. This research analyzed U.S. military and economic aid data to search for significant changes in the amount of aid given to Israel and Egypt during this time period. The changes in aid amount were then correlated to historical events to provide the strategic context for the flux in U.S. foreign aid given to the two countries. The declassified documents of the *Foreign Relations of the United States (FRUS)* for this time period were reviewed to identify the U.S. foreign policy objectives associated with the U.S. foreign aid given to Israel and Egypt. The resulting responses of Israel and Egypt were identified to infer the effectiveness of using U.S. foreign aid at achieving the U.S. foreign policy objectives. A review of U.S. foreign aid to Israel and Egypt is provided as background, followed by a review of the FRUS historical documentation to identify the U.S. foreign policy objectives for the aid given and the resulting responses from Israel and Egypt. Finally, factors that may have impacted the effectiveness of using U.S. foreign aid as a tool of U.S. foreign policy are discussed.

U.S. Foreign Aid to Israel

After World War II, international support for an independent Israeli state intensified in response to the near-extermination of European Jewry by the Nazis.[22] However, both Palestinians and Jewish refugees resided on a relatively small piece of contested land on the coast of the Mediterranean that was once known as Palestine. On November 29, 1947, the United Nations General Assembly passed Resolution 181 to endorse a plan to partition Palestine into separate Jewish and Arab states with Jerusalem under United Nations control. After declaring its independence in 1948, Israel was promptly invaded by its Arab neighbors trying to defend the remaining Palestinians residing in the newly declared Israeli state. The fighting lasted from May to December 1948 when an armistice was reached between Israel and its Arab neighbors that left Israel in control of three quarters of the former Palestine.

Israel is the largest cumulative recipient of U.S. aid since World War II and was the

---

[22] U.S. Department of State, "Background Note: Israel, February 22, 2012," http://www.state.gov/r/pa/ei/bgn/3581.htm#relations (accessed on March 15, 2012).

largest annual recipient of U.S aid from 1976-2004, having been supplanted by Iraq.[23] U.S. assistance to Israel began in 1949 with a $100 million Export-Import Bank loan.[24] Israel also received assistance from France, which was also Israel's weapons supplier even as the United States agreed to sell Hawk anti-aircraft missiles to Israel in 1962. After Israel's success in the Six Day War, the United States agreed to sell McDonnell Douglas F-4 Phantom II aircraft to Israel, beginning a long-standing relationship with the United States to ensure that Israel maintained a qualitative military edge over its neighbors.[25] In 2008, the U.S. Congress passed U.S. Public Law 110-429, Section 201 (the Naval Transfer Act of 2008) that defined qualitative military edge as

> the ability to counter and defeat any credible conventional military threat from any individual state or possible coalition of states or from non-state actors, while sustaining minimal damages and casualties, through the use of superior military means, possessed in sufficient quantity, including weapons, command, control, communication, intelligence, surveillance, and reconnaissance capabilities that in their technical characteristics are superior in capability to those of such other individual or possible coalition of states or non-state actors.[26]

Further, the law amended Section 36 of the Arms Export Control Act requiring an evaluation of all proposed sale or export of defense articles or services to any country in the Middle East in order to determine whether the sale or export would adversely affect Israel's qualitative military edge in the region. Ensuring Israel's qualitative military edge is at the foundation of the U.S. security commitment to Israel.[27]

From 1971 to 2012, U.S. aid to Israel averaged approximately $2.6 billion per year, two-thirds of which was military assistance.[28] In the mid-1990s, Israel and the United States agreed to reduce the amount of economic aid provided to Israel.[29] By fiscal year 1999, the U.S. Congress had reduced the amount of economic assistance for Israel by $120 million dollars per year and increased the amount of Foreign Military Financing (FMF) by $60 million dollars per

---

[23] Jeremy M. Sharp, *U.S. Foreign Aid to Israel*, Washington, DC: U.S. Library of Congress, Congressional Research Service: Report for Congress, March 12, 2012, i.

[24] Ibid, 27.

[25] Sharp (2012), 27.

[26] *Naval Vessel Transfer Act of 2008*. Public Law 110-429, 110th Congress, 2nd Session (October 15, 2008).

[27] U.S. Department of State, "Ensuring Israel's Qualitative Military Edge," http://www.state.gov/t/pm/rls/rm/176684.htm (accessed 4 September 2012).

[28] Sharp (2012), 28.

[29] Sharp (2012), 3.

year.30 By fiscal year 2008, Israel was no longer receiving economic assistance since it had advanced to a self-sustaining industrialized economy, in part due to U.S.-Israel scientific cooperation that led to advances in Israel's high-tech sector.31 In 2007, the George W. Bush administration and Israel agreed to a 10 year, $30 billion military aid package that would raise Israel's annual FMF from approximately $2.55 billion in fiscal year 2009 to approximately $3.1 billion in fiscal year 2013 through fiscal year 2018.[32] For fiscal year 2013, the Barack Obama administration requested $3.1 billion of FMF grants and $15 million in migration and refugee funds.[33] Israel is the largest recipient of U.S. FMF grants.[34] Israel has also received funds of varying amounts to assist in the resettlement of refugees and immigrants to the country since 1973.[35]

In addition to U.S. military financial assistance, Israel also receives advanced military systems and military training as well as participates in joint exercises and personnel exchanges.[36] For example, in 2010, Israel and the United States participated in a missile defense exercise named Juniper Cobra, with more than 1,000 U.S. personnel involved in the exercise. To defend against rocket attacks from Hamas in the Gaza Strip, in fiscal year 2011, the Obama administration requested $205 million, in addition to already allocated FMF amounts, to support Iron Dome, a short-range anti-rocket system. Further, the United States and Israel jointly developed the Arrow Anti-Missile System to protect against medium to long-range missile threats from hostile entities in Lebanon, Syria, and Iran. Also in 2010, the United States and Israel announced that Israel would purchase 19 F-35s, the fifth generation stealth aircraft considered to be the most technologically advanced fighter jet ever made, for $2.75 billion to be paid using FMF grants.[37] Israel is also part of the War Reserves Stock Allies-Israel program in which the United States stores missiles, armored vehicles, and artillery ammunition on Israeli bases for use during wartime.[38] Israel can request permission to use the U.S. war reserve

---

[30] Clyde R. Mark, *Israel: U.S. Foreign Assistance*, Washington, DC: Library of Congress, Congressional Research Service, April 26, 2005), 3.

[31] Jeremy M. Sharp, *U.S. Foreign Aid to Israel*, Washington, DC: Library of Congress, Congressional Research Service, September 16, 2010, 2.

[32] Sharp (2012), i.

[33] Ibid.

[34] Sharp (2012), 6.

[35] Sharp, (2012), 20.

[36] U.S. Department of State, "Ensuring Israel's Qualitation Military Edge," http://www.state.gov/t/pm/rls/rm/176684.htm (accessed 4 September 2012).

[37] Sharp (2012), 7.

[38] Sharp (2012), 15.

stockpile in a military emergency.[39]

With respect to other financial benefits as part of the U.S.-Israel relationship, the United States provides loan guarantees to Israel, which enable Israel to borrow from commercial sources at lower rates; Israel has never defaulted on a U.S.-backed loan guarantee and Israel has not borrowed any funds since fiscal year 2005.[40] On July 27, 2012, President Obama signed the U.S.-Israel Enhanced Security Cooperation Act, which included an extension of the loan guarantees for Israel until September 2015.[41] According to U.S. Public Law 108-11, Israel is required to use the loan within the pre-June 5, 1967 borders, i.e. not in the West Bank, including East Jerusalem or the Gaza Strip.[42] The law also stipulates that the United States may reduce or deduct the amount of funds Israel used in areas outside of the pre-1967 borders. For example, on November 26, 2003, $289.5 million was deducted from the total $3 billion loan guarantee because Israel was building settlements in the West Bank and the Gaza Strip and the security barrier separating Israelis and Palestinians.[43] For fiscal year 2005, the United States deducted another $795.8 million from the remaining loan amount available to Israel. In lesser amounts, for fiscal years 2000-2011, the U.S. Congress provided approximately $39 million for the American Schools and Hospital program, administered by the U.S. Agency for International Development, designed to support schools, libraries, and medical centers that demonstrate American ideals and practices abroad.[44] In addition, the U.S. Congress has authorized funds to support U.S.-Israeli bilateral foundations to stimulate industrial and scientific research.[45]

U.S. Foreign Aid to Egypt

U.S. security and economic assistance to Egypt expanded significantly after the 1979 peace treaty between Israel and Egypt. Since 1979, Egypt has been the second largest recipient of U.S. foreign assistance after Israel and remains in the top five recipient of U.S. aid received

---

[39] Ibid.

[40] Sharp (2012), 21.

[41] *United States-Israel Enhanced Security Cooperation Act of 2012*. 112th Congress, 2nd Session, Public Law 112-150 (July 27, 2012).

[42] *Emergency Wartime Supplemental Appropriations Act, 2003*. Public Law 108-11, 108th Congress, 1st Session (April 16, 2003).

[43] Sharp (2012), 21.

[44] Sharp (2012), 24.

[45] Sharp (2012), 25.

and requested in fiscal years 2012 and 2013, respectively.[46] Assistance from the United States for Egypt is geared toward development of its economy and military.[47] Egypt receives the majority of U.S. aid in the form of FMF, Economic Support Funds (ESF) and International Military Education and Training (IMET).[48] According to the U.S. General Accounting Office (GAO), Egypt uses its FMF funds to acquire new equipment, upgrade existing equipment, and for follow-on support and maintenance contracts.[49] Since 1979, Egypt has received approximately $34 billion in FMF assistance, in the annual amount of approximately $1.3 billion.[50] Further, the GAO assessed that U.S. FMF assistance accounted for 80 percent of Egypt's military budget and has enabled Egypt to replace outdated Soviet-supplied equipment with modern U.S. equipment. As of 2005, through the FMF program, Egypt has purchased 36 Apache helicopters, 220 F-16 aircrafts, 880 M1A1 Abrams battle, tanks, and the associated training and maintenance support for these systems, among other equipment.[51] The M1A1 Abrams battle tanks are part of a joint production program that started in 1988 in which a percentage of the tank components are manufactured in Egypt while the remaining parts are produced in the United States and shipped to Egypt for assembly.[52]

Economic aid for Egypt is distributed to a variety of projects and sectors such as health, education, economic growth and democracy and governance.[53] In the late 1990s, the U.S. Congress wanted to reduce the amount of economic aid to Israel and Egypt over a ten-year period.[54] While military aid to Israel increased during this period, Egypt did not receive an increase in military assistance as economic aid decreased. Economic aid decreased from $815 million in fiscal year 1998 to $411 million in fiscal year 2008 and $200 million in fiscal year 2009. A small increase in economic aid, $50 million, was allocated to Egypt for fiscal year 2010 when President Obama assumed office. While a relatively small portion of the total economic aid

---

[46] Jeremy M. Sharp, *Egypt: Transition under Military Rule*, Washington, DC: Library of Congress, Congressional Research Service (June 12, 2012), 15 and 22.

[47] U.S. Department of State, "U.S. Relations with Egypt," http://www.state.gov/r/pa/ei/bgn/5309.htm (accessed September 5, 2012).

[48] Sharp, Egypt: Transition under Military Rule, 15.

[49] U.S. Government Accounting Office. Security Assistance: State and DOD Need to Assess How the Foreign Military Financing Program for Egypt Achieves U.S. Foreign Policy and Security Goals, GAO 06-437. Washington, DC: General Accounting Office, 2006, 10.

[50] GAO, 8.

[51] Ibid.

[52] Sharp, Egypt: Transition under Military Rule, 15.

[53] Ibid, 17.

[54] Ibid, 16.

package for Egypt, funds allocated toward promotion of democracy in Egypt have been a controversial topic. Former Egyptian President Hosni Mubarak objected to U.S. economic aid given to support democracy promotion programs, demanding prior approval from any foreign government for such programs to function in country.[55] To counter Mubarak's demands, the Consolidated Appropriations Act of 2005 stipulated that organizations funded by U.S. aid to promote democracy, human rights and governance do not require prior approval from the Egyptian Government.[56] This exemption language on promotion of democracy is generalized to state that "organizations implementing such assistance and the specific nature of that assistance shall not be subject to the prior approval by the government of any foreign country" in the Consolidated Appropriations Act of 2012, Section 7034(h)(3).[57]

Due to the uncertainty in government and leadership in Egypt as a result of the Arab Spring revolution, proposed legislation appropriating U.S. aid to Egypt included certain conditions for the new Egypt. For fiscal year 2013, the Department of State, Foreign Operations, and Related Programs Appropriation Bills introduced by the U.S. House of Representatives (H.R. 5857) and the U.S. Senate (S.3241), respectively, included stipulations that require the Secretary of State to certify that Egypt had met its obligations under the 1979 Egypt-Israel Peace Treaty before funds could be distributed.[58] In addition, the Secretary of State must certify that Egypt has transitioned to democratically elected and civilian controlled government that will protect human rights and civil liberties. H.R. 5837 requested $259 million in ESP and $1.3 billion in FMF. S.3241 requested the same amount of ESF and FMF, minus the amount of bail posted in February 2012 for members of nongovernmental organizations arrested in Egypt. Both bills have yet to be voted on by the U.S. Congress as of August 2012. While the U.S. Congress considers the fiscal year 2013 appropriation legislation, a Gallop poll showed that 82 percent of Egyptians surveyed opposed the United States sending economic aid to Egypt, as of February 2012.[59] There was no reference to military aid in the poll.

---

[55] Ibid, 17.

[56] *Consolidated Appropriations Act, 2005.* Public Law 108-447, 108th Congress, 2nd Session (December 8, 2004).

[57] *Consolidated Appropriations Act, 2012.* Public Law 112-74, 112th Congress, 1st Session (December 23, 2011).

[58] *Department of State, Foreign Operations, and Related Programs Appropriations Act, 2013.* H.R.5857, Section 7042(a), and S.3241, Section 7041 (b), 112th Congress, 2nd Session (May 24 and 25, 2012).

[59] Mohamed Younis and Ahmed Younis, "Egyptian Opposition to U.S. and Other Foreign Aid Increases, March 29, 2012," http://www.gallup.com/poll/153512/egyptian-opposition-foreign-aid-increases.aspx (accessed September 5 2012).

Historical Examples

U.S. Foreign Aid Trends

The historical dollar amount (not adjusted for inflation) of total U.S. military and economic aid is plotted as a function of fiscal year from the 1952-1969 (figure 1). The U.S. military aid data compiled by USAID did not delineate the type of military aid given to the recipient, only a total amount.[60] The amount of economic aid is a total amount allocated to various programs recorded by the USAID data for ease of representation in the graph. The graph showed that U.S. economic aid to Israel was generally consistent ranging from a low of approximately $6 million in 1967 during the Six Day War to a high of approximately $86 million in 1952. Significant U.S. military aid for Israel of approximately $13 million appeared in 1962, to coincide with the U.S. agreement to sell Hawk missiles to Israel. U.S. military aid for Israel dramatically increased to approximately $96 million in 1966, when the United States agreed to sell the Skyhawk combat aircraft to Israel.[61] The amount of U.S. military aid to Israel was decreased to approximately $7 million in 1967 during the Six Day War and then increased again in 1969 to approximately $85 million, when Israel received its first Phantom fighter aircraft.

U.S. economic aid given to Egypt increased substantially in 1955 to approximately $66 million; decreased to approximately $33 million in 1956; and a low of approximately $601,000 in 1958 following the Suez Canal Crisis in 1956. In 1959, the United States raised the amount of economic aid given to Egypt to approximately $45 million, until a high of approximately $200 million in 1962. The amount of U.S. economic aid decreased the following years until a low of approximately $13 million in 1967 during the Six Day War. No economic aid data were recorded for 1968 and 1969. Due to the lack of details on how the U.S. foreign aid was allocated or from what source or legislation, the aid amount may not be indicative of all aid given to Israel and Egypt. The graph is a qualitative analysis intended to show trends in U.S. foreign aid given to both countries during the 1950s to 1960s in order to provide a focus in the FRUS review.

---

[60] U.S. Agency for International Development, "U.S. Overseas Loans and Grants: Obligations and Loan Authorizations, July 1, 1945-September 30, 2010," http://gbk.eads.usaidallnet.gov/ (accessed September 2012).

[61] Zach Levey, "The United States' Skyhawk Sale to Israel, 1966: Strategic Exigencies of an Arms Deal," *Diplomatic History* 28, no. 2 (April 2004).

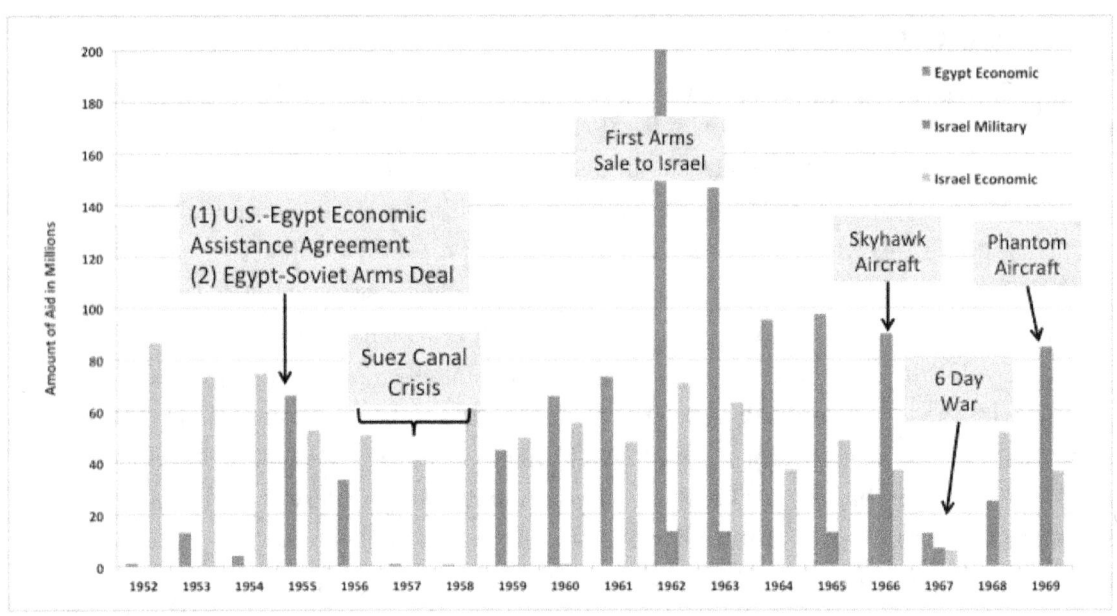

U.S. Foreign Aid to Israel and Egypt 1952-1969

Figure 1. U.S. foreign aid given to Israel and Egypt during 1952-1969. Significant historical events are noted to correspond to increases or decreased in aid amount. *Source*: USAID data. Graph created by author.

Aid as Tool of Influence on Israel

Historical precedence showed that the United States used foreign aid a tool of persuasion or coercion to balance the Israeli and Arab power struggle in the region. In June

1957, Israeli Minister of Finance Eshkol appealed for additional aid from the United States as a result of the new financial burden of handling the large influx of Jewish immigrants from Poland, Hungary and Egypt.[62] While Secretary of State John Foster Dulles expressed sympathy toward Israel's plight, he cautioned that Israel "should be under no illusions as to the prospects of assistance" from the United States.[63] Further, Dulles stated to Eshkol that the United States was sensitive to Arab concerns regarding the increased immigration and its implications for Israel's territorial expansion. In response to Israel's request for more aid, Assistant Secretary of State for Near Eastern, South Asian, and African Affairs, William M. Roundtree, noted that the provision of additional assistance to Israel would raise tensions with Arab states in the region.[64] During this time, Israel had finally withdrawn forces from the Gaza Strip and the Sinai in the wake of the Suez Canal crisis. Roundtree noted that Israel's financial difficulties were the result of the military campaign against Egypt and immigration, both of which were policies opposed by the United States. Roundtree recommended against giving additional aid to Israel because he was concerned that the United States would appear to be rewarding Israel for withdrawing forces as well as complicate efforts to strengthen relations with friendly Arab states (Jordan, Lebanon, Saudi Arabia, and Iraq). A few months prior, in a March 1957 internal memorandum, Roundtree believed that the Israelis were well aware of the U.S. position against large-scale immigration and therefore, declining to increase economic aid to Israel was probably "the most effective way of making [the] point with the Israelis."[65]

Based on the previous documentation outlining U.S. government officials stated intention toward Israel, economic aid was used curb Israeli territorial expansion and to mitigate Arab sensitivities to the immigration issue. However, from the Israeli perspective, the State of Israel was the first and most important priority. While Israel often claimed that aid was an economic and security necessity during meetings with U.S. officials, Israeli actions showed that Israel would risk losing the money rather than compromise its agenda. On Israel's immigration

---

[62] Memorandum of a Conversation, Department of State, Washington, June 24, 1957, *Foreign Relations of the United States, 1955–1957, Volume XVII, Arab-Israeli Dispute.* Document 345. (Washington, DC: Department of State), http://history.state.gov/historicaldocuments/frus1955-57v17/d345 (accessed September 2, 2012. Hereafter FRUS Online).

[63] Ibid.

[64] Memorandum From the Assistant Secretary of State for Near Eastern, South Asian, and African Affairs Rountree to the Deputy Under Secretary of State for Economic Affairs Dillon, June 20, 1957. FRUS Online, 1955–1957 Volume XVII, Arab-Israeli Dispute, Document 343, http://history.state.gov/historicaldocuments/frus1955-57v17/d343 (accessed September 2, 2012).

[65] Memorandum From the Assistant Secretary of State for Near Eastern, South Asian, and African Affairs Rountree to the Acting Secretary of State, March 13, 1957. FRUS Onine, 1955–1957; Volume XVII, Arab-Israeli Dispute, Document 219, http://history.state.gov/historicaldocuments/frus1955-57v17/d219 (accessed September 3, 2012).

influx, Foreign Minister Golda Meir stated that it was impossible to change the policy on immigration since the State of Israel was created to provide a homeland for the Jewish people.[66] Recognizing U.S. fears of rising tension with Arab neighbors, Meir stated that she had repeated publicly that Israel had no further territorial expansion, often to deaf ears however. In this manner, Meir was able to appease U.S. sensitivities while staying true to the identity of Israel as a Jewish homeland.

Keeping true to its priority to protect the Jewish homeland, security requirements were a consistent reason cited by Israel for aid requests from the United States. During a meeting with Dulles in October 1958, Meir expressed Israel's deep fear of being encircled by aggressors and requested U.S. assistance to acquire 55 Patton tanks from the United Kingdom.[67] Meir added that Israel did not have the money to pay for the tanks. Dulles replied that the United States preferred to concentrate on economic assistance rather than become a major arms supplier to Israel. In another example, during a September 1960 meeting with Department of State officials, Israeli Minister of Finance Levi Eshkol noted that the Israeli Ministry of Defense was pressing for double the previous expenditure levels.[68] Eshkol requested additional special assistance funds to compensate for the security expense and offered financing of private housing as a channel to funnel the additional aid from the United States. However, Acting Secretary of State Douglas C. Dillon cautioned that there were political objections to aid for housing because of the immigration issue. Eshkol admitted that he had resisted increases in security expenditures that may be wasteful, but was caught in a difficult position when he was serving David Ben-Gurion who was Israel's prime Minister as well as the minister of defense.

To Ben-Gurion, Israel's survival depended on military assistance in aid and equipment from the United States. During a May 30, 1961 meeting with President John F. Kennedy, Ben-Gurion tried to convince President Kennedy to provide the Hawk anti-aircraft missiles to Israel for defensive purposes against Egypt. Ben-Gurion told President Kennedy, "if [Egypt] should

---

[66] Memorandum of a Conversation, Ambassador Eban's Residence, Washington, October 12, 1957. FRUS Online, 1955–1957; Volume XVII, Arab-Israeli Dispute, Document 383, available online at http://history.state.gov/historicaldocuments/frus1955-57v17/d383 (accessed September 3, 2012).

[67] Memorandum of a Conversation, Department of State, Washington, October 2, 1958. FRUS Online, 1958–1960; Volume XIII, Arab-Israeli Dispute; United Arab Republic; North Africa, Document 39, http://history.state.gov/historicaldocuments/frus1958-60v13/d39 (accessed September 3, 2012).

[68] Memorandum of a Conversation, Department of State, Washington, September 20, 1960. FRUS Online, 1958–1960; Volume XIII, Arab-Israeli Dispute; United Arab Republic; North Africa, Document 169, http://history.state.gov/historicaldocuments/frus1958-60v13/d169 (accessed September 3, 2012).

defeat us they would do to the Jews what Hitler did."[69] Kennedy responded that while United States supported Israel's security, the United States did not want to contribute to an escalation of weaponry in the region. Ben-Gurion's view of Israel's security position with respect to Egypt was not shared by the Department of State and the Department of Defense. The Department of Defense had concluded that Israel maintained an overall advantage over Egypt, according to an internal Department of State memorandum.[70] The internal memorandum added that Israel enjoyed superiority in leadership, morale, organization, training, logistics, maintenance and intelligence. In an August 1960 letter to Ben-Gurion, Secretary of State Christian A. Herter had explained that the United States did not want to become an arms supplier in the region but admitted that the large amount of financial aid provided to Israel had contributed to Israel's ability to shoulder the defense burden, including the purchase of military requirements from other suppliers.[71] Ben-Gurion, on the other hand, saw the situation much differently and was "deeply disappointed" by the U.S. recalcitrance in providing arms to Israel at this time.[72] While Israel continued to receive economic aid from the United States during this period, Ben-Gurion no longer saw it as sufficient to ensuring Israel's security. Ben-Gurion wanted advanced weaponry from the United States.

By mid-1962, relations between Israel and the United States had deteriorated, partly due to U.S. refusal to sell the Hawk missiles to Israel as well as Israel's objection to U.S. attempts to resolve the long-standing issue of how to handle Palestinian refugees since the inception of the State of Israel. Under President Kennedy, the United States wanted to resolve the Palestinian refugee problem as a step toward Arab-Israel peace.[73] In addition, the U.S. Congress was calling for a reduction of financial commitments to the United Nations Relief and Work

---

[69] Memorandum of Conversation, May 30, 1961. FRUS Online, 1961–1963; Volume XVII, Near East, 1961–1962, Document 57, http://history.state.gov/historicaldocuments/frus1961-63v17/d57 (accessed September 3, 2012).

[70] Memorandum from the Assistant Secretary of State for Near Eastern and South Asian Affairs Talbot to Secretary of State Rusk, November 22, 1961. FRUS Online, 1961–1963; Volume XVII, Near East, 1961–1962, Document 143, http://history.state.gov/historicaldocuments/frus1961-63v17/d143 (accessed September 3, 2012).

[71] Letter From Secretary of State Herter to Prime Minister Ben Gurion. August 4, 1960. FRUS Online, 1958–1960; Volume XIII, Arab-Israeli Dispute; United Arab Republic; North Africa, Document 163, http://history.state.gov/historicaldocuments/frus1958-60v13/d163 (accessed September 3, 2012).

[72] Memorandum of a Conversation, Washington, August 18, 1960. FRUS Online, 1958–1960; Volume XIII, Arab-Israeli Dispute; United Arab Republic; North Africa, Document 165, http://history.state.gov/historicaldocuments/frus1958-60v13/d165 (accessed September 3, 2012).

[73] Memorandum From Secretary of State Rusk to President Kennedy. August 7, 1962. FRUS Online, 1961–1963; Volume XVIII, Near East, Document 15, http://history.state.gov/historicaldocuments/frus1961-63v18/d15 (accessed September 3, 2012).

Agency for Palestinian Refugees in the Near East, which had totaled approximately $300 million, $25 million annually and increasing steadily. Dr. Joseph E. Johnson was appointed as a Special Representative of the United Nations Palestine Conciliation Commission in August 1961 to develop a plan to resolve the refugee issue. Dr. Johnson had finished his proposal by August 7, 1962. At the same time, the Department of State conducted a review of the U.S policy toward Israel, noting Israel's desire to seek a close military relationship, a security guarantee, and access to a wider range of military equipment from the United States, specifically the Hawk missile.[74]

The Kennedy administration needed to gain Israel's support for the Johnson initiative. On August 9, 1962, Assistant Secretary of State for Near Eastern and South Asian Affairs Phillips Talbot proposed sending a Presidential Emissary to secure Israel's cooperation for the Johnson Plan.[75] Talbot noted that the U.S. resolve on the "quid pro quo" should be firm, including the Hawk missile as part of a deal to obtain Ben-Gurion's pledge of cooperation in Johnson's plan and assurances that Israel would not introduce a resolution proposing direct negotiations between Israel and its Arab neighbors at the United Nations General Assembly. On August 19, 1962, Myer Feldman, deputy special counsel to the president, informed Ben-Gurion and Israeli Foreign Minister Golda Meir that President Kennedy had agreed to sell the Hawk missile to Israel.[76] During the same meeting, Feldman broached the Johnson Plan with Ben-Gurion and Meir, who responded negatively to the proposal with Ben-Gurion insisting on certain guarantees from Egypt before acquiescing to the Johnson Plan. Secretary of State Rusk stressed to Feldman that "it would be most unfortunate if [the] Israelis were to end up with the Hawks and strengthened security assurances while being responsible for derailing the Johnson Plan before it could even be given a good try."[77]

After subsequent meetings, Feldman was able to obtain a secret agreement from Meir that Israel would not introduce the direct negotiations resolution at the United Nations General

---

[74] Memorandum From Secretary of State Rusk to President Kennedy. August 7, 1962. FRUS Online, 1961–1963; Volume XVIII, Near East, Document 14, http://history.state.gov/historicaldocuments/frus1961-63v18/d14 (accessed September 3, 2012).

[75] Memorandum From the Assistant Secretary of State for Near Eastern and South Asian Affairs Talbot to the President's Deputy Special Counsel Feldman. August 9, 1962. FRUS Online, 1961–1963; Volume XVIII, Near East, Document 17, http://history.state.gov/historicaldocuments/frus1961-63v18/d17 (accessed September 3, 2012).

[76] Telegram From the Embassy in Israel to the Department of State, August 19, 1962. FRUS Online, 1961–1963; Volume XVIII, Near East, Document 24, http://history.state.gov/historicaldocuments/frus1961-63v18/d24 (accessed September 3, 2012).

[77] Telegram From the Department of State to the Embassy in Israel, August 20, 1962. FRUS Online, 1961–1963; Volume XVIII, Near East, Document 25, http://history.state.gov/historicaldocuments/frus1961-63v18/d25 (accessed September 3, 2012).

Assembly and further, Israel would "not say anything" to obstruct implementation of the Johnson Plan unless Egypt jeopardizes the issue.[78] However, not saying anything did not equate to acceptance of the Johnson Plan as Israel continued to oppose the Johnson Plan, leading to the United States to abandon support of the proposal.[79] Further clouding the Israeli position, by October 1962, Feldman had learned that Israel was circulating the direct negotiations resolution at the United Nations, in apparent reversal of an earlier promise not to introduce the resolution.[80] Feldman called Israeli Ambassador to the United States Avraham Harman for an explanation. Harman stated that Israel was forced to take certain measures, such as the direct negotiations resolution, as a result of the Johnson Plan to ensure that Israel maintained some leverage on the refugee issue. Harman added that if the United States did not insist on the Johnson Plan, then Israel would not need to introduce the direct negotiations resolution to the United Nations. Having already obtained the Hawk missile agreement, Israel was bargaining with the United States from a position of strength and reneged on the previous agreement not to introduce the direct negotiations resolution to the United Nations.

Israeli actions with respect to the Johnson Plan and the Hawk missile agreement showed that Israel was looking out for itself first. In this case, Israel was able to out-maneuver the United States into providing the Hawk missiles without having to commit to the Johnson Plan on Palestinian refugees, which was strongly opposed by Israel. U.S. officials used the incentive of the Hawk missiles to gain Israeli support for the Johnson Plan, a leverage that was lost after the Hawk missile sale agreement. Israel mounted "an all-out effort to sink the Johnson Plan," leading U.S. officials scrambling to contain the political damage by attempting to lay the onus of the failure on the Arabs and Israelis, rather than "appearing to cave ourselves."[81] The agreement to sell Hawk missiles to Israel was an important milestone in the U.S.-Israel relationship, the first of what would become a long-standing military cooperation relationship between the two countries. This example also showed that Israel would readily reverse

---

[78] Memorandum of Conversation, August 24, 1962. FRUS Online, 1961–1963; Volume XVIII, Near East, Document 30, http://history.state.gov/historicaldocuments/frus1961-63v18/d30 (accessed September 3, 2012).

[79] Circular Telegram From the Department of State to Certain Posts, September 26, 1962. FRUS Online, 1961–1963; Volume XVIII, Near East, Document 56, http://history.state.gov/historicaldocuments/frus1961-63v18/d56 (accessed September 3, 2012).

[80] Memorandum From the President's Deputy Special Counsel Feldman to President Kennedy, October 2, 1962. FRUS Online, 1961–1963; Volume XVIII, Near East, Document 64, http://history.state.gov/historicaldocuments/frus1961-63v18/d64 (accessed September 3, 2012).

[81] Memorandum From Robert W. Komer of the National Security Council Staff to the President's Deputy Special Assistant for National Security Affairs Kaysen, September 22, 1962. FRUS Online, 1961–1963, Volume XVIII, Near East, Document 52, http://history.state.gov/historicaldocuments/frus1961-63v18/d52 (accessed September 3, 2012).

whatever position was promised behind closed doors if the issue could jeopardize Israel's sovereignty, such as the Palestinian refugees. Israel wanted to ensure that it controlled how many and in what manner Palestinian refugees would be repatriated to Israel as part of any negotiations on the issue, something which Israel believed was not guaranteed by the Johnson Plan.[82] Israel won this round by forcing the United States to abandon the Johnson Plan while also boosting its security with acquisition of the Hawk missiles.

By late 1965, Israel was pressuring the United States to agree to sell combat aircrafts to Israel after exhausting other Western supplier and in light of Egypt's acquisition of MIG-21s, Sukhoi low-level attack planes, TU-16 bombers and helicopters.[83] As part of a Memorandum of Understanding to gain Israel's acceptance for an U.S. arms deal to Jordan in March 11, 1965, the United States had agreed to "ensure an opportunity for Israel to purchase a certain number of combat aircraft, if not from Western sources, then from the United States.[84] Negotiations for the combat aircraft continued in February 1966 when Secretary of Defense Robert S. McNamara met with Israeli Foreign Minister Eban to detail conditions for Israel before the United States would agree to sell the Skyhawk A-4 aircraft.[85] As conditions, McNamara stated that Israel (1) would not oppose U.S. aircraft sale to Jordan; (2) would not be the first to develop nuclear weapons in the Middle East and accept periodic inspection of the Dimona nuclear facility; and (3) agree to full secrecy until the United States decided otherwise. On March 31, 1966, Israel accepted the U.S. conditions but referred to the agreement as "affirmations of Israeli policy, rather than as conditions tied strictly to an aircraft sale."[86] Israel also insisted on no written agreement, fearing history would show that Israel had "bargained away [its] future nuclear

---

[82] Memorandum From the Assistant Secretary of State for Near Eastern and South Asian Affairs Talbot to Secretary of State Rusk, September 20, 1962. FRUS Online, 1961–1963, Volume XVIII, Near East, 1962–1963, Document 48, http://history.state.gov/historicaldocuments/frus1961-63v18/d48 (accessed September 3, 2012).

[83] Memorandum of Conversation, December 29, 1965. FRUS Online, 1964–1968; Volume XVIII, Arab-Israeli Dispute, Document 260, http://history.state.gov/historicaldocuments/frus1964-68v18/d260 (accessed September 3, 2012).

[84] Telegram From the Embassy in Israel to the Department of State, March 11, 1965, FRUS Online, 1964–1968; Volume XVIII, Arab-Israeli Dispute, Document 185, http://history.state.gov/historicaldocuments/frus1964-68v18/d185 (accessed September 3, 2012).

[85] Memorandum of Conversation, February 12, 1966. FRUS Online, 1964–1968; Volume XVIII, Arab-Israeli Dispute, Document 271, http://history.state.gov/historicaldocuments/frus1964-68v18/d271 (accessed September 3, 2012).

[86] Memorandum From the Assistant Secretary of Defense for International Security Affairs McNaughton to Secretary of Defense McNamara, March 31, 1966. FRUS Online, 1964–1968; Volume XVIII, Arab-Israeli Dispute, Document 283, http://history.state.gov/historicaldocuments/frus1964-68v18/d283 (accessed September 3, 2012).

policy and opened the Dimona facility to US inspection for the sake of a mere 48 airplanes."[87]

Mounting Arab-Israel tensions culminated in the Six Day War, beginning with an Israeli attack on Egyptian airfields and Jordanian and Syrian air force on June 5, 1967, followed by land offensive into the Gaza Strip and the Sinai Peninsula that overwhelmed Egyptian forces, and Israeli defeat of Jordanian and Syrian land forces.[88] A cease-fire was reached on June 10, 1967 and Israel gained control of East Jerusalem, the West Bank, the Gaza Strip, the Sinai, and the Golan Heights. At the onset of the war by June 7, 1967, the United States immediately suspended all aid obligations to the region, including Israel.[89] Suspension of military aid continued until Secretary of Defense Rusk requested and was approved for selective relaxation of arms shipment to Arab states and Israel in October 13, 1967.[90] By December 1967, Israel was alarmed by the rapid Soviet resupply of the Arab air force. Israeli Ambassador to the United States Avraham Harman reported that the Egypt, Syria, Iraq, and Algeria had 550 fighter aircrafts and 62 bombers against Israel's total of 155 aircrafts.[91] Israel was requesting "27 additional A-4 Skyhawks to be delivered in 1969 on top of the 48 that will be delivered in 1968 and 50 F-4 Phantoms for delivery in 1969-70."[92]

Negotiations throughout 1968 for the Phantom aircraft coincided with discussion of Israel's position on the Non-Proliferation Treaty (NPT) as the United States tried to obtain clarity on Israel's nuclear weapons plans and whether it would sign the NPT.[93] Israel had maintained an ambiguous position on the NPT. In a June 1968 letter to Secretary of State Rusk, Israeli

---

[87] Ibid.

[88] Anne M. Lesch and Dan Tschirgi, *Origins and Development of the Arab-Israeli Conflict* (Westport, CT: Greenwood Press, 1998). 20.

[89] Memorandum for the Record, National Security Council Meeting, Wednesday, June 7, 1967. FRUS Online, 1964–1968; Volume XIX, Arab-Israeli Crisis and War, Document 194, http://history.state.gov/historicaldocuments/frus1964-68v19/d194 (accessed September 3, 2012).

[90] Memorandum From Secretary of State Rusk to President Johnson, October 13, 1967. FRUS Online, 1964–1968; Volume XIX, Arab-Israeli Crisis and War, Document 472, http://history.state.gov/historicaldocuments/frus1964-68v19/d472 (accessed September 3, 2012).

[91] Telegram From the Department of State to the Embassy in Israel, December 9, 1967. FRUS Online, 1964–1968; Volume XX, Arab-Israeli Dispute, Document 11, http://history.state.gov/historicaldocuments/frus1964-68v20/d11 (accessed September 3, 2012).

[92] Memorandum From the President's Special Assistant Rostow to President Johnson, December 13, 1967. FRUS Online, 1964–1968; Volume XX, Arab-Israeli Dispute, Document 19, http://history.state.gov/historicaldocuments/frus1964-68v20/d19 (accessed September 3, 2012).

[93] Telegram From the Department of State to the Embassy in Israel, October 24, 1968. FRUS Online, 1964–1968; Volume XX, Arab-Israeli Dispute, Document 288, http://history.state.gov/historicaldocuments/frus1964-68v20/d288 (accessed September 3, 2012).

Foreign Minister Abba Eban explained that Israel "supported the principle of non-proliferation of nuclear weapons ... but the draft treaty cannot in itself give us a sense of assurance that nuclear weapons will never become available to our neighbours—particularly as not all the nuclear powers are associated with the treaty."[94]

Israel objected strongly to the perception that the NPT and Phantom negotiations were linked and stated that the "NPT and the planes are two separate issues; let's get on with the planes."[95] President's Special Assistant Walt W. Rostow advised President Johnson that Israel was deliberately pressuring the United States to separate the Phantom negotiations from the NPT and the United States would have to pursue Israel and the NPT separately in order to conclude the Phantom negotiations promptly.[96] Negotiations were concluded by November 27, 1968, with an announcement that the United States agreed to sell 50 F-4 Phantom aircrafts and related equipment and services to Israel.[97] Further as part of the agreement, Israel reiterated its commitment as outlined in the Memorandum of Understanding of March 11, 1965, that Israel would "not be the first power in the Middle East to introduce nuclear weapons and [agreed] not to use any aircraft supplied by the United States as a nuclear weapons carrier."[98]

U.S. concerns regarding Israel's nuclear ambitions coincided with negotiations to sell advanced combat aircrafts, the Skyhawk and the Phantom, to Israel. In addition, balancing and countering Soviet influence in the Arab states were important factors for the U.S. agreement to sell the Skyhawk and Phantom aircrafts to Israel. Both agreements were in response to increased military support provided by the Soviet Union to Egypt and the United States wanted to ensure that Israel maintained an advantage to Egypt. Further, the U.S. arms deal to Jordan added another armed Arab state to the region which led to the Skyhawk sale agreement for Israel, thus ensuring Israel's military advantage. Throughout, the United States declared that it was following a policy of not becoming a major arms supplier in the Middle East but the Skyhawk and the Phantom were exemptions to this policy to counter Soviet influence in the

---

[94] Telegram From the Embassy in Israel to the Department of State, July 2, 1968. FRUS Online, 1964–1968; Volume XX, Arab-Israeli Dispute, Document 205, http://history.state.gov/historicaldocuments/frus1964-68v20/d205 (accessed September 3, 2012).

[95] Action Memorandum From the President's Special Assistant Rostow to President Johnson, October 25, 1968, FRUS Online, 1964–1968; Volume XX, Arab-Israeli Dispute, Document 290, http://history.state.gov/historicaldocuments/frus1964-68v20/d290 (accessed September 3, 2012).

[96] Ibid.

[97] Letter from the Assistant Secretary of Defense for International Security Affairs Warnke to the Israeli Ambassador Rabin, November 27, 1968. FRUS Online, 1964–1968; Volume XX, Arab-Israeli Dispute, 1967–68, Document 333, http://history.state.gov/historicaldocuments/frus1964-68v20/d333 (accessed September 3, 2012).

[98] Ibid.

Arab states. The U.S. arms deal to Jordan was a calculated risk to provide limited arms in order to keep Jordan from turning to the Soviet Union for arms supply.[99] Nevertheless, by this arms deal, the United States had armed another country in the Middle East and Israel gained the Skyhawk combat aircraft, and as a result, the United States had become an arms supplier and escalated the arms race in the region. The sale of Skyhawk and Phantom aircrafts to Israel allowed the United States to balance the Soviet-armed Egypt and arming Jordan allowed the United States to avert further Soviet influence in the region.

The United States was able to obtain a concession by Israel's assurance that it would not use U.S. aircraft to carry nuclear weapons but Israel obfuscated its position on the NPT and its intentions on developing nuclear weapons. Israel has not signed the NPT. Surrounded by perceived hostile neighbors, Israel would not give up the nuclear security blanket. And in the examples of the Skyhawk and Phantom acquisitions, Israel did not have to give in to U.S. pressure on the nuclear issue to get the aircrafts in the end. Israel's priority to protect the Jewish homeland remained consistent in the negotiations for the Hawk anti-aircraft missiles and the Skyhawk and Phantom combat aircrafts. The historical precedence showed that Israel has always looked out for itself, first and foremost in its foreign policy priorities.

Aid as Tool to Counter Communism in Egypt

Like the Marshall Plan, countering communist influence in the Middle East was one of the objectives in the U.S. strategy of providing foreign aid to Egypt. Since the early 1950s, the United States had provided various forms of aid to Egypt in order to maintain a cooperative relationship with the regime.[100] For example, Egypt received $10 million as part of a technical assistance program that ended in March 1953. The United States concluded an economic assistance agreement with Egypt on November 6, 1954 and $40 million of economic assistance was allocated in fiscal year 1955 for Egypt. However, the United States had to that point refrained from providing military assistance to Egypt. By mid-1955, there were signs that Egypt sought to purchase arms from the Soviet Union. In a June 1955 meeting with U.S. Ambassador to Egypt Henry A. Byroade, Egyptian Prime Minister Gamal Abdul Nasser made clear that the morale of the Egyptian army and the security of Egypt required additional military equipment.

---

[99] Memorandum From President Johnson to the Under Secretary of State for Political Affairs Harriman and Robert W. Komer of the National Security Council Staff, February 21, 1965. FRUS Online, 1964–1968; Volume XVIII, Arab-Israeli Dispute, Document 157, http://history.state.gov/historicaldocuments/frus1964-68v18/d157 (accessed September 3, 2012).

[100] Telegram from the Department of State to the Embassy in Egypt, July 9, 1956. FRUS Online, 1955–1957; Volume XV, Arab-Israeli Dispute, January 1–July 26, 1956, Document 434, http://history.state.gov/historicaldocuments/frus1955-57v15/d434 (accessed September 3, 2012).

Nasser had not committed to acquiring arms from the Soviet Union while he waited for Washington's decision on whether to sell arms to Egypt. Nasser claimed that he could make a deal in which the Russians would not be allowed inside Egypt and that communism in Egypt could be controlled.[101] Not long after the meeting with Byroade, Nasser finalized an arm deal with Czechoslovakia (of the Soviet Union bloc) on September 27, 1955.[102]

In response, Under Secretary of State Herbert Hoover, Jr. drafted a letter to Nasser, on behalf of Secretary of State John Foster Dulles, seeking an explanation for the Egyptian-Soviet arms deal. The letter stated that the United States

> extended [economic] assistance...in the belief that [it] would make possible close cooperation with the West...[and that the] proposed agreement with the Soviet Union inevitably undermines the basic premise upon which we have worked in the past and sets Egypt upon a course which may well separate her progressively from her natural and long-term friends.[103]

This letter implied that the United States was expecting Egypt to align with the West against the Soviet Union in return for economic assistance. However, Nasser had gained prestige and position in the Arab world as a result of the Soviet arms deal and was determined to maintain his new position, according to a Central Intelligence Agency (CIA) assessment.[104] The CIA added that if the United States provided more aid to Egypt, neighboring countries would expect similar increases in assistance from the United States.

By mid-July, 1956, the United States was beginning to view Egyptian policies and relations with the Soviet Union as detrimental to U.S. objectives. On July 17, 1956, Assistant Secretary for Near Eastern, South Asian, and African Affairs George V. Allen recommended that the United States withdraw financial support to the Aswan High Dam project in Egypt.[105] Allen

---

[101] Telegram From the Embassy in Egypt to the Department of State, June 17, 1955. FRUS Online, 1955–1957; Volume XIV, Arab-Israeli Dispute, Document 132, http://history.state.gov/historicaldocuments/frus1955-57v14/d132 (accessed September 2, 2012).

[102] Lesch and Tschirgi, 14.

[103] Telegram From the Secretary of State to the Department of State, September 27, 1957. FRUS Online, 1955–1957; Volume XIV, Arab-Israeli Dispute, Document 315, http://history.state.gov/historicaldocuments/frus1955-57v14/d315 (September 3, 2012).

[104] Telegram From the Director of Central Intelligence Dulles, October 29, 1955. FRUS Online, 1955–1957; Volume XIV, Arab-Israeli Dispute, Document 369, http://history.state.gov/historicaldocuments/frus1955-57v14/d369 (accessed September 3, 2012).

[105] Memorandum From the Assistant Secretary of State for Near Eastern, South Asian, and African Affairs Allen to the Secretary of State, July 17, 1956. FRUS Online, 1955–1957; Volume XV, Arab-Israeli Dispute, January 1–July 26, 1956, Document 467, http://history.state.gov/historicaldocuments/frus1955-57v15/d467 (accessed September 3, 2012).

believed that Nasser was driven by his own vision of "Egypt's destiny" and was attempting to extract the most gain from the West-East struggle, with the West on the losing end of this game. Allen assessed that applying pressure, such as withdrawing support for the Aswan High Dam, would convey to Nasser the dangers of playing the West against the Soviet Union. Allen hoped that Nasser's position would be weakened by this action because Nasser had promised the success of the Aswan High Dam to the Egyptian people, claiming that he could gain favors from both the West and the Soviet Union without repercussions. In this manner, Allen was using the withdrawal of financial aid as a means of punishment for Nasser's collaboration with the Soviet Union. Allen added that the United States should make clear to Egypt that any other type of assistance was contingent on cessation of Egyptian actions contrary to Western interests.

Not long after withdrawing support for the Aswan High Dam project, Nasser, who was also president, seized control of the Suez Canal Company on July 26, 1956. In a two and a half hour speech regarding the Egyptian nationalization of the Suez Canal Company, Nasser criticized the West for the "no strings" support to Israel and added that in contrast, the Soviet Union had offered long-term loans with no conditions attached.[106] By February 1957, The U.S. stopped all arms and aviation shipment to Egypt and the U.S. Treasury froze Egyptian assets in the U.S. Technical and economic development programs for Egypt were allowed to taper off and no new programs were underway.[107] During a February 15, 1957 meeting on the state of U.S.-Egypt relations, U.S. Ambassador to Egypt Raymond A. Hare found Nasser to be defensive and evasive, with Nasser referring to U.S. actions, such as freezing Egyptian assets and suspension of aid programs, to be unfriendly and not indicative of good intentions toward Egypt.[108] Nasser claimed that he had no choice but to turn to the Soviet Union for economic assistance if cut off from the West. In essence, the Suez Canal crisis created a vacuum in which the Soviet Union was able to exert influence on Egyptian foreign policy that was detrimental to U.S.-Egypt relations.

Nasser's belief that he could contain the Soviet influence in Egypt and get what he

---

[106] Telegram From the Embassy in Egypt to the Department of State, July 26, 1956. FRUS Online, 1955–1957; Volume XV, Arab-Israeli Dispute, January 1–July 26, 1956, Document 511, http://history.state.gov/historicaldocuments/frus1955-57v15/d511 (accessed September 3, 2012).

[107] Memorandum by the Deputy Director of the Office of Near Eastern Affairs Rockwell and by Lewis Hoffacker of that Office, February 19, 1957. FRUS Online, 1955–1957; Volume XVII, Arab-Israeli Dispute, 1957, Document 119, http://history.state.gov/historicaldocuments/frus1955-57v17/d119 (accessed September 3, 2012).

[108] Memorandum by the Officer in Charge of Israel–Jordan Affairs, Officer of Near Eastern Affairs, Department of State Donald C. Bergus, March 8, 1957. FRUS Online, 1955–1957; Volume XVII, Arab-Israeli Dispute, 1957, Document 206, http://history.state.gov/historicaldocuments/frus1955-57v17/d206 (accessed September 3, 2012).

wanted from both the United States and the Soviet Union limited the use of U.S. aid as a counter to communist influence in the country. If Nasser did not get what he wanted from the United States, he turned to the Soviet Union instead, which Nasser believed had no strings attached unlike the aid from the United States. The party line Nasser gave to U.S. officials was that Egypt was neutral, not choosing between the United States and the Soviet Union. In hindsight, Nasser appeared to be naïve to believe that he could balance Egypt's relationship with both the United States and the Soviet Union, or that support from the Soviet Union had no string attached. Alternatively, Nasser's overriding ambition to be the leader of the Arab Unity movement forced him to assume the risk of alienating the United States for the prestige gained by the Soviet arms deal and other forms of support. By 1958, Nasser had the advantage of being at the pinnacle of his popularity and no other pro-Western Arab leader in the region could compete with Nasser's appeal.[109]

Post-Suez Canal crisis, U.S. aid to Egypt began to rise, with a substantial increase in fiscal year 1962 due to urgent Egyptian requests as a result of a crop disaster in 1961. According to Robert W. Komer, senior staff at the National Security Council, in a memorandum to President John F. Kennedy, by 1962, the aims of the United States in providing aid to Egypt were to:

> (a) provide Nasser with some alternative to total dependence on the Bloc; (b) help turn [Egypt] energies inward, as has seemed to be happening after Syrian coup; (c) give Nasser some vested interest in good relations with us—and by inference with our allies; and (d) help reassure Nasser that the US, while not endorsing his policies, is not actively hostile. In essence, our aid has been part of a long-term strategy toward an important neutralist state, still the most influential in the Arab world.[110]

Maintaining some engagement with Egypt by continuing to provide aid appeared to have succeeded to some degree. On December 9, 1967, Nasser requested passage of a formal message to President Lyndon B. Johnson in which Nasser expressed regret for his past speeches accusing the United States of conducting a "war of starvation" on Egypt.[111] Further, Nasser

---

[109] Memorandum from the Assistant Secretary of State for Near Eastern, South Asian, and African Affairs Rountree to Secretary of State Dulles, March 24, 1958. FRUS Online, 1958–1960; Volume XII, Near East Region; Iraq; Iran; Arabian Peninsula, Document 14, http://history.state.gov/historicaldocuments/frus1958-60v12/d14 (accessed September 3, 2012).

[110] Memorandum From Robert W. Komer of the National Security Council Staff to President Kennedy, February 15, 1962. FRUS Online, 1961–1963; Volume XVII, Near East, 1961–1962, Document 192, http://history.state.gov/historicaldocuments/frus1961-63v17/d192 (accessed September 3, 2012).

[111] Telegram from the U.S. Interests Section of the Spanish Embassy in the United Arab Republic to the Department of State, December 10, 1967. FRUS Online, 1964–1968; Volume XX, Arab-Israeli Dispute, 1967–68, Document 13, http://history.state.gov/historicaldocuments/frus1964-68v20/d13 (accessed September 3, 2102).

claimed that he made these inflammatory statements to please the Soviets.

Despite being critical of Egypt's policies and objectives, the United States did not cut off all support to Egypt in order to leave open the possibility for a more favorable engagement later. The United States opted to wait out Nasser's ambitions, assessing that Nasser's drive for domination would cause problems and obstacles for himself down the road.[112] A May 1966 National Intelligence Estimate assessed that Egypt's "need for Western aid will be an important but not overriding consideration in its conduct of foreign affairs."[113] In this way, the United States knowingly accepted the risk of allowing Nasser to grow in prominence, under Soviet Union's patronage, with the expectation that Nasser and Egypt would need the United States at a later time.

Conclusion

The U.S. policy on providing foreign aid follows the three theories of international relations; i.e. liberal internationalism, constructivism, and realism. The United States provided foreign aid to Egypt for humanitarian and ideological reasons when Egypt suffered a crop disaster in 1961 and to Israel when it declared its independence as a Jewish state after surviving attempted genocide at the hands of the Germans during World War II. This is in line with the constructivist motivation for foreign aid. However, the United States also used foreign aid to strengthen international institutions such as the World Bank and to increase development in countries, enabling the spread of globalization. This follows the liberal internationalist thought for use of foreign aid. Economic assistance is the primary form of aid to promote the constructivist and liberal internationalist view of foreign aid, while military aid is the realist rationale for providing foreign aid to a recipient. For example, the United States provided military aid to Israel in order to strengthen an important ally in the region and to Jordan in order to prevent another Arab country from turning to the Soviet Union like Egypt had in the 1955 arms deal.

U.S. foreign aid is accepted as a fundamental part of U.S. foreign policy, and as Morgenthau envisioned, an instrument of national power on par with the military and

---

[112] Memorandum From the Assistant Secretary of State for Near Eastern, South Asian, and African Affairs Rountree to Secretary of State Dulles, March 24, 1958. FRUS Online, 1958–1960; Volume XII, Near East Region; Iraq; Iran; Arabian Peninsula, Document 14, http://history.state.gov/historicaldocuments/frus1958-60v12/d14 (accessed September 3, 2012).

[113] National Intelligence Estimate, May 19, 1966. FRUS Online, 1964–1968; Volume XVIII, Arab-Israeli Dispute, Document 290, http://history.state.gov/historicaldocuments/frus1964-68v18/d290 (accessed September 3, 2012).

diplomacy. Since 1970s, Israel and Egypt have been among the top five recipients of U.S. foreign aid. Israel and Egypt are important partners for the United States in maintaining stability in the Middle East, as reflected by the large amount of U.S. foreign aid given to both countries. Since 2008, by law, the United States committed to assisting Israel in maintaining a qualitative military edge over its neighbors and all proposed military sale or export to the region must be evaluated to determine the risk of jeopardizing Israel's qualitative military edge. Therefore, U.S. foreign policy for the Middle East, especially with respect to Israel, is greatly influenced by this commitment to Israel's qualitative military edge in the region, in direct and indirect ways. For example, Israel is the largest recipient of U.S. FMF while U.S. relations with Arab neighbors have to bear in mind the risk to Israel's security.[114] For Egypt, given the uncertainties as a result of the Arab Spring Revolution, the U.S. Congress is considering legislation for fiscal year 2013 foreign aid appropriations which includes stipulations requiring the Secretary of State to certify that Egypt has transitioned to a democratically elected, civilian controlled government that protects and guarantees human rights and civil liberties, prior to release of funds.[115]

A review of historical documents of the foreign relations of the United States for Egypt and Israel during the 1950s and 1960s showed that the United States attempted to use foreign aid to maintain influence with Israel and Egypt as well as to counter communism in the region. The United States provided economic aid to both Israel and Egypt during this time period with significant U.S. military aid given to Israel beginning in 1962 with the sale of Hawk anti-aircraft missiles. This was followed by the sale of the Skyhawk and Phantom combat aircrafts to Israel in 1966 and 1969, respectively. The sale of the advanced combat aircrafts was the beginning of a long-standing tradition of military cooperation between Israel and United States to ensure that Israel maintained a qualitative military edge over its neighbors. In Egypt, the United States provided economic aid for humanitarian and political reasons. Egypt's desire to modernize its military and to assume a leadership role in the Arab Unity movement allowed the Soviet Union to gain influence by supplying arms and support to Egypt. In response, the United States used economic aid as way to remain engaged with Egypt even as its policies, influenced by the Soviet Union, were contrary to U.S. objectives. At the same time, the United States increased military aid to Israel to counter-balance the Soviet arming of Egypt as well as agreed to an arms deal with Jordan in order to prevent additional Soviet arms and influence in the region.

In addition to countering Soviet influence in the region, U.S. foreign aid was used as an incentive to persuade Israel to curb its territorial expansion and large-scale acceptance of Jewish

---

[114] Sharp (2012) and the *Naval Vessel Transfer Act of 2008*. Public Law 110-429, 110th Congress, 2nd Session (October 15, 2008).

[115] *Department of State, Foreign Operations, and Related Programs Appropriations Act, 2013.* H.R.5857, Section 7042(a), and S.3241, Section 7041 (b), 112th Congress, 2nd Session (May 24 and 25, 2012).

immigrants, which aggravated Arab sensitivities of "Zionist ambitions." However, while claiming that it did not have further territorial ambitions, Israel adhered to its immigration policy, citing its identity as a Jewish homeland. Further, U.S. foreign policy objectives could not overcome Israel's priority to put its national identity and security above the amount of U.S. foreign aid received. When U.S. foreign policy objectives for the aid were at opposition to Israel's political agenda, Israel was able to out-maneuver, delay, and finally outlast the United States during the negotiations for key military aid that Israel considered necessary for its security. For example, Israel was able to acquire the Hawk anti-aircraft missile, the Skyhawk aircraft, and the Phantom aircraft without having to commit to the Johnson plan or give up its nuclear ambitions.

For Egypt, the United States had to compete with the Soviet Union as an aid source, allowing Egypt to gain the advantage in its engagements with the United States. If Egypt did not like the strings attached to U.S. foreign aid, Egypt turned to the Soviet Union. Egyptian President Nasser claimed neutrality between the Soviet Union and the United States. However, Nasser's ambition, and overriding animosity toward Israel and the perceived carte blanche of U.S. support for Israel, led Nasser to deepen Soviet-Egyptian ties throughout the 1950s and 1960s. The incentive of U.S. foreign aid had little influence on directing Egyptian policies away from the Soviet Union toward the United States.

Returning to Morgenthau's political theory of foreign aid, the historical examples of Israel and Egypt showed that foreign aid was an ineffectual tool of foreign policy when the priorities of the giver and the recipient are not aligned. In the current era of fierce budget battles and escalating deficits in the United States, calls to cut foreign aid are renewed due to the perception that the foreign aid has not succeeded in promoting U.S. interests abroad. Following Morgenthau's realist perspective on international relations, the United States should recognize that other countries would always place their national interests first in priority. Therefore, the interests of the recipient are equally important when the United States consider using foreign aid to achieve a foreign policy objective. No amount or type of aid would convince the recipient to take a position in opposition to its identity or national interests. For foreign aid to succeed in gaining political loyalties from the recipient, the United States must persuade the recipient to adopt the position of the United States. Foreign aid alone cannot accomplish this goal but it is attainable when foreign aid is used along with diplomacy and military means, the trifecta of U.S. national power.

Bibliography

Brainard, Lael. Security by Other Means: Foreign Assistance, Global Poverty, and American Leadership. Washington, DC: Brookings Institution Press, 2006.

Caruson, Kiki and Farrar-Myers, Victoria A. "Promoting the President's Foreign Policy Agenda: Presidential Use of Executive Agreements as Policy Vehicles." *Political Research Quarterly* 60, no. 4 (December 2007), 631-644.

Consolidated Appropriations Act, 2005. Public Law 108-447, 108th Congress, 2nd Session (December 8, 2004).

Consolidated Appropriations Act, 2012. Public Law 112-74, 112th Congress, 1st Session (December 23, 2011).

Cosmas, Graham A. MACV: The Joint Command in the Years of Escalation, 1962-1967, United States Army in Vietnam. Washington, DC: United States Army Center of Military History, 2006.

Department of State, Foreign Operations, and Related Programs Appropriations Act, 2013. H.R.5857, Section 7042(a) and S.3241, Section 7041 (b), 112th Congress, 2nd Session (May 24 and 25, 2012).

Emergency Wartime Supplemental Appropriations Act, 2003. Public Law 108-11, 108th Congress, 1st Session (April 16, 2003).

Khadka, Narayan. "U.S. Aid to Nepal in the Cold War Period: Lessons for the Future." *Pacific Affairs* 73, no. 1 (Spring 2000), 77-95.

Lai, Brian. "Examining the Goals of US Foreign Assistance in the Post-Cold War Period, 1991-96." *Journal of Peace Research* 40, no. 1 (January 2003), 103-128.

Lancaster, Carol. *Foreign Aid: Diplomacy, Development, Domestic Politics*. Chicago, IL: University of Chicago Press, 2006.

Lancaster, Carol and Van Dusen, Ann. *Organizing U.S. Foreign Aid: Confronting the Challenges of the 21st Century*. Washington, DC: Brookings Institution Press, 2005.

Lesch, Anne M. and Tschirgi, Dan. *Origins and Development of the Arab-Israeli Conflict*. Westport, CT: Greenwood Press, 1998.

Levey, Zach. "The United States' Skyhawk Sale to Israel, 1966: Strategic Exigencies of an Arms Deal." *Diplomatic History* 28, no. 2 (April 2004): 255-276.

Mark, Clyde R. *Israel: U.S. Foreign Assistance*. Washington, DC: Library of Congress, Congressional Research Service, April 26, 2005.

Meernik, James, Krueger, Eric L., Poe, Steven C. "Testing Models of U.S. Foreign Policy: Foreign Aid during and after the Cold War." *The Journal of Politics* 60, no. 1 (February 1998), 63-85.

Morgenthau, Hans. "Introductions." In *The New Statecraft* by George Liska, iv. Chicago; Univeristy of Chicago Press, 1960.

_____. "A Political Theory of Foreign Aid" *The American Political Science Review* 56, no. 2 (June 1962), 301-309.

Naval Vessel Transfer Act of 2008. Public Law 110-429, 110th Congress, 2nd Session (October 15, 2008).

Obama, Barack. *National Security Strategy*. Washington, DC: The White House, 2010.

Office of the U.S. President. "Fact Sheet: U.S. Global Development Policy, September 22, 2010." http://www.whitehouse.gov/the-press-office/2010/09/22/fact-sheet-us-global-development-policy (accessed September 5, 2012).

Poe, Steven C. and Meernik, James. "US Military Aid in the 1980s: A Global Analysis." *Journal of Peace Research* 32, no. 4 (November 1995), 399-411.

Sharp, Jeremy M. *Egypt: Transition under Military Rule*. Washington, DC: Library of Congress, Congressional Research Service (June 12, 2012).

_____. *U.S. Foreign Aid to Israel*. Washington, DC: Library of Congress, Congressional Research Service, September 16, 2010.

_____. *U.S. Foreign Aid to Israel*. Washington, DC: U.S. Library of Congress, Congressional Research Service: Report for Congress, March 12, 2012.

United States Agency for International Development. "U.S. Overseas Loans and Grants: Obligations and Loan Authorizations, July 1, 1945-September 30, 2010." http://gbk.eads.usaidallnet.gov/ (accessed September 2012).

United States Congress. *Congressional Record*. 103rd Congress, 1st Session, March 19, 1993. Vol. 139, No. 35: S3240-S3242. http://thomas.loc.gov/cgi-bin/query/D?r103:368:./temp/~r103Ydml6Z::(accessed October 11, 2012).

United States Department of State. "Background Note: Israel, February 22, 2012." http://www.state.gov/r/pa/ei/bgn/3581.htm#relations (accessed on March 15, 2012).

_____. "Ensuring Israel's Qualitative Military Edge." http://www.state.gov/t/pm/rls/rm/176684.htm (accessed 4 September 2012).

_____. "Fact Sheet: U.S.-Relations with Egypt, August 22, 2012." http://www.state.gov/r/pa/ei/bgn/5309.htm (accessed September 6, 2012).

_____. "FY 2013 Executive Budget Summary - Function 150 and Other International Programs, February 13, 2012." http://www.state.gov/s/d/rm/rls/ebs/2013/index.htm (accessed October 11, 2012).

_____. *Foreign Relations of the United States (FRUS): 1955–1957; Volume XIV, Arab-Israeli Dispute, 1955*. Washington, DC: Department of State. http://history.state.gov/historicaldocuments (accessed September 3, 2012).

_____. Foreign Relations of the United States: 1955–1957; Volume XV, Arab-Israeli Dispute, January 1–July 26, 1956.

_____. Foreign Relations of the United States: 1955–1957, Volume XVII, Arab-Israeli Dispute, 1957.

_____. Foreign Relations of the United States: 1958–1960; Volume XII, Near East Region; Iraq; Iran; Arabian Peninsula.

_____. Foreign Relations of the United States: 1958–1960; Volume XIII, Arab-Israeli Dispute; United Arab Republic; North Africa.

_____. Foreign Relations of the United States: 1961–1963; Volume XVII, Near East, 1961-1962.

_____. Foreign Relations of the United States: 1961–1963; Volume XVIII, Near East, 1962-1963.

_____. Foreign Relations of the United States: 1964–1968; Volume XVIII, Arab-Israeli Dispute.

_____. Foreign Relations of the United States: 1964–1968; Volume XIX, Arab-Israeli Crisis and War.

_____. Foreign Relations of the United States: 1964–1968; Volume XX, Arab-Israeli Dispute.

_____. Foreign Relations of the United States: 1964–1968; Volume XX, Arab-Israeli Dispute, 1967–68.

_____. "U.S. Relations with Egypt." http://www.state.gov/r/pa/ei/bgn/5309.htm (accessed September 5, 2012).

United States Government Accounting Office. Security Assistance: State and DOD Need to Assess How the Foreign Military Financing Program for Egypt Achieves U.S. Foreign Policy and Security Goals, GAO 06-437. Washington, DC: General Accounting Office, 2006.

United States-Israel Enhanced Security Cooperation Act of 2012. 112th Congress, 2nd Session, Public Law 112-150 (July 27, 2012).

Wang, T. Y. "U.S. Foreign Aid and UN Voting: An Analysis of Important Issues." International Studies Quarterly 43, no. 1 (March 1999), 199-210.

Younis, Mohamed and Younis, Ahmed. "Egyptian Opposition to U.S. and Other Foreign Aid Increases, March 29, 2012." http://www.gallup.com/poll/153512/egyptian-opposition-foreign-aid- increases.aspx (accessed September 5 2012).